Hold Them Close

Hold Them Close

Sarah Agnew

RESOURCE *Publications* • Eugene, Oregon

HOLD THEM CLOSE

Copyright © 2018 Sarah Agnew. All rights reserved. Except for brief quotations in critical publications or reviews, no part of this book may be reproduced in any manner without prior written permission from the publisher. Write: Permissions, Wipf and Stock Publishers, 199 W. 8th Ave., Suite 3, Eugene, OR 97401.

Resource Publications
An Imprint of Wipf and Stock Publishers
199 W. 8th Ave., Suite 3
Eugene, OR 97401

www.wipfandstock.com

PAPERBACK ISBN: 978-1-5326-5503-6
HARDCOVER ISBN: 978-1-5326-5504-3
EBOOK ISBN: 978-1-5326-5505-0

Manufactured in the U.S.A.

Contents

Fragmented

now. a day. | 2
to breathe | 3
A lonely fragment | 4
the colour penitent | 5
Dragon's tears | 6
out of the mouths | 7
Sing on | 9
defiant company | 10
unhappy | 11
to be. wanting | 12
unseen | 13
mus musculus | 14
November dark, November light | 16
precipitous | 17
The Haar | 18
Sacred whisper | 19

Closer

uncommon joy | 22
Before the dawn | 23
in two places, I wish | 24
the solitary | 25
edging closer | 26
but it never happened | 27
you are loved | 28
Breath/Prayer | 29
Defiance | 30
a generous turn | 31

Two Foot London Lament | 33
on the bus: 1 | 34
A New Aunt's Gaze | 35
museum of art: impression | 36
Nanna's House | 37
on being found | 38
Into One Spirit | 39
Joy to the whole world | 40

Dream

Perchance | 42
when my own voice falters | 43
For she has been a benefactor to many | 44
if one falls in the Forest of Dreams | 45
hung out | 46
her heart's not in it | 47
Resignation. | 48
average | 50
taking all you've granted | 51
Observing the trees: Autumn | 52
a prophet's homecoming | 53
chase the wild goose | 54
I am ready | 55
carried: home | 56

Acknowledgements

Some poems in this collection have previously been published on the author's blog: sarahtellsstories.blogspot.com, or in recorded versions at soundcloud.com/sarahtellsstories. 'chase the wild goose' was composed by request during, and as part of, worship at Greyfriars Kirk, Edinburgh, Pentecost 2016.

I publish these poems with gratitude for the stories, people, and Spirit, who inspired so many of them, and who demonstrate again and again that we are only fully human with each other.

Fragmented

now. a day.

the sun shimmers,
but today I cannot shine.
the songs of the birds dance
to my ears, but my heart
will not join them, not
today.
the children play,
but, oh today, this does
not evoke, not even
a glimmer.

my blue eyes are but faded
watermark
today.
my heart's strings are stretched
and snapped and smack
the bars of its cage,
on repeat,
and repeat,
repeat.
my lips are a salt bed
in the shimmering sun
today, cracked edges peeled
back on a silent cave,
today.

to breathe

When I look at the glass and see
the curves the world would deem
unpretty, I look again, for in
these curves are asides
the pills have cast, a story
and a struggle with unbalance and
disorder;
        beneath them lies the strength
required to crawl towards the light.

These curves, this body is alive—
conclusion not foregone, and not
forgotten, the beauty
of the choice

A lonely fragment

the edges of my happy wrinkle,
burnt with the flame of sad, a light
remembered in a darkened room;
I had you near a short, sweet time—
The End came from far, too soon.

my happy is torn in many places,
holes and gaps and empty spaces;
you, and they, and here, and now,
wrapped raggedness with sacred leaves,
a holy cover holding tight
for a while.

could we but rest a moment
longer within that blissful binding if
this book could only be
the only story in your library?

but suddenly, or seemingly, it is
undone,
        you are gone, and I,
                once more,
                        am all

the colour penitent

purple teardrops
falling from the sky

purple raindrops
make puddles in my eyes

purple scarlines
invisible, inside

purple wine drops
spill over all denial

Dragon's tears

gay | gei | adjective : "lighthearted and carefree"

is anyone lighthearted, do
you think, at one small group
declaring for all the manner in
which we are to be happy?

can anyone be carefree, now
with humanity broken on
the dance floor, in a happy
place turned flooded bath?

will anyone be happy again, smile
again, laugh again? has all the gay
gone from the world? or will
it land in our midst, a giant dragon
with expansive tail bending love around
the mountain?

out of the mouths

1.

On a Paris street,
in a morning walk, they stop
to talk to the camera:
Papa, I am scared.
Of what, my child?
Of the angry people
and their angry guns—what if
they come back again?
Then we will lay more flowers,
my child; we will always
have more flowers.

2.

In a home Down Under,
on the way to slumber, they stop
for a pressing question:
Mum, what will happen
when there is no more room?
No more room for what,
my child? What if—
there is no more room for all
the bodies, to put them when
they need rest?
Then we will dig deeper,
my child, we will find
a way to go deeper still.

3.

In an ancient never ending story,
Ramah wails again; lamentation
covers the bodies, bomb-dust
and fire smoke, stifling cover, suffocation,
smother—
Rachels kneel unseen among the stones,
in the fallen shell-shocked ruins
of life made empty; Rachels
who will not be consoled, refuse
flowers for the burden grief will lay
upon them, must lay within
them, deeper, so much
deeper than humans ought to dig.
There are no streets, no graves, no
children asking *what if*—
only Rachels' weeping[1] turning
dust to restless mud.

---

1. "A voice is heard in Ramah, mourning and great weeping, Rachel weeping for her children and refusing to be comforted, because they are no more." (Jeremiah 31:15; cf. also Matthew 2:18)

Sing on

An ode to Manchester. 23.05.17

Petals bled their white
and red, from roots
buried deep under hearth
of home; but the Song
outgrew the Roses.

Streets and theatres burst
exploding from a spark
buried not so far from hearth
and home; but the Song
drowned out the Blitz.

City centre blast
to rubble, the cord
buried within the hearth
of home; but the Song
outlasted the Troubles.

Small shadows flicker
light eclipsed, the switch
buried by the hearth
of home; but the Song
will outshine Terror.

defiant company

*for those who sat beside me through a dark and stormy day,
reaching love across time and space*

what will the black dog take
from this encounter, this latest
attempt to stand, to deliver blow
and plunder all the joy and life from deep
inside?

what will the black dog take
from meeting human shields and swords
of light that shimmer through the mist
it hissed in my direction?

the black dog will not take
wounds to bind or lick;
its life
       it will retain.
but it will not be permitted to take from me more
space than it was given, will not make
of its corner a residence to call
its own.

as light fades a world away, it has been sent
to stand guard around me, a cobbled rampart
drawn from other lives and generations.

what will the black dog take from me,
scrape from the flesh beneath its claws?
a lesson will it take, a message sounding up
from empty jaws and un-pricked ears –
*hear this, black dog foe, black
dog companion, this one here is loved, is not
alone—*
       should you choose to rise again, know this:
Sarah is defended.

unhappy

your "I love you" weaves
a rug to briefly hang above
this bed then sink, then render
breathless—I pull
away from weighted strands
appealing, ephemeral, I
run to make my lungs
expand, shake off the spell
you cast—you used to
make me less

to be. wanting

I don't want to be happy
I don't want to be sad
I don't want to be angry
I don't want to be mad

I don't want to be green
I don't want to be blue
I don't want to be me
I don't want to be you

I don't want to stay in
I don't want to go out
I don't want to be puffed up
I don't want to be let down

I don't want to be here
I don't want to be there
I don't want to know when?
I don't want to go—where?

I don't want to be here
I don't want to feel
I don't want not to
I don't want . . . to

unseen

off-white grey shrouding
invisibility falls:
the black dog rises

mus musculus

it's just a mouse
but my cat-like hearing
has no meaning now, without
a cat's budding taste for
the kill.
a mouse
in my one-room flat
full of gaps just right
for a mouse's
doorway
and it does like
to scratch away at them, clamber
through them right when I
am sleeping; but my cat's
ears don't sleep, no, they catch
every claw sound and paw
strike across the floor
as that mouse
explores my books and bags
and boxes in the corners;
just a little mouse,
but in the dark I'm under
siege and cannot reach
for sleep with muscles
and tendons spring-like
to—cat-like—pounce!
if I didn't shudder at the thought
of that mouse
getting anywhere near
me; that mouse
surely jeers at my peppermint
coating of its door
ways, my gentle coaxing it out
of my flat—there are no
food scraps or bread

buns or rolls shedding their
crusts—that's one way to
get me to clean, let
a mouse
in—
get that mouse
out!
if I didn't shudder
at the thought of taking
a life, even the life of an itty
little mouse,
that mouse
would be out
and I
might
sleep.

November dark, November light[2]

it is the darkest corner of the world,
but we do not believe that darkness
buries every light, so where we are
we'll burn the wicks, stoke the fires,
and turn our faces toward that dark
corner, to see the shadows
flickering in our flames, to see
small light looking back at us; we
will look, eyes open on our freedom
incomplete while humans are not free;
we will not turn away from what we cannot
see, for we are braver in greater
numbers; flash and sparkle in the sky,
blaze and crackle on the beach;
flicker, shimmer, quietly on
the table—most of all,
shine, shine, shine, and so unite
our hearts with those who live inside
the darkest corner of the world.

---

2. Written after #alightforaleppo, awareness movement initiated by University of Edinburgh Chaplaincy.

precipitous

we cast our votes
amid the lies flinging
fear slinging torrent
and the rain fell
bleak teller of fortune

we watched the count
amid hope sliding
faith sinking avalanche
and the rain fell
gentle persistent soundtrack

we heard the echoes
amid our own stunned
speechless shock
and the rain fell
as if nothing at all had changed

The Haar

damp curtain, off-white
silent wave from ocean sky
pulled across the glass

Sacred whisper

for Jason

I'll light a ring of candles,
place them side by side;
a ring of flames to flicker
at the edges of the dark.

And in the vacancy of feeling,
when tempest eye is open
above the ocean depths of who you are,
I hope you'll listen and you'll see:

I lit a ring of little candles,
set them, side by side, upon the edges,
to flutter hopeful, mutter love—
full and spilling light into the dark.

Closer

uncommon joy

pale grey canopy
split second gashes of light
Nature's laughter deep

to weeping delight
showering upon steamy
earth cool relief

throw the curtain back
blink warm up for heavy eyes
your summer day: made

Before the dawn

you. in dreaming. this morning's
waking, forever friend of time
long past. an embrace beyond
every day hellos. we hugged,
sat down to dinner. your wife,
your friends of now—her I liked,
but them—I play another tune. we
laughed, your eyes shone as I
remembered.
               what are we
doing here, in clouds before
the dawn?
               what is this apparition?
longing for connection, or
affection, fulfilled in imagination? truth
revealed? I miss you, miss
the friendships of our youth; I feel far
from home, from well-known. promise?
sign or guidance—new direction—new
wish—to finish the solo, join
a band, clasp hands?
                       What will I find
when dawn arrives,
                    clears away the mist?

in two places, I wish

to walk this sand with you,
fingers barely touching in
the heat;

to shower trinkets over you, treasures
from places I felt your presence
from afar;

to drink this beer with you,
its taste of home I cannot describe
in words;

to talk and hear you talk
beyond imagined reconnection

the solitary

sometimes
wants a hand
to hold, a neck to
nuzzle into, lips
to kiss your forehead,
arms to fold around
your torso, a torso
to hold in your arms,
skin against skin, scent
to breathe in, fingers to
weave in your hair; to stare
through those windows open
the windows to your own—
hand it back, hand
in mine, fingers inter-
twined, not mine alone—
but only

edging closer

summer sky rumbles,
evoking a knowing smile—
nature's power, Divine
reminder of human
speck of milky dust;
my joy reaches to the threshold
of your sleepless night
on a kindling bed,
cracking floor a spark
away from roaring
tide that will roll under
cloud uprising—let your
worry reach to the threshold
of my damp airbed
on a borrowed floor,
awake to all
I will miss

but it never happened

he wrote
would you like to go to lunch?

she wrote
yes. are we to be friends, now?

he wrote
I was
asked at dinner where
my thoughts were roaming:
unguarded
for that moment I answered,
with someone I met, walked
in step with, naturally, talked in
truth with, openly—I was surprised
to uncover this lingering there
in my thoughts with another. so lunch
is more a date—if that's OK?

she wrote
I smile as I read your words—I
have been surprised to think
of another, such comfort I thought
I had found, alone; I am glad
to make it a date, that you
have spoken, for I would have let
you go and always
wondered:

you are loved

for Ruby

I looked for words
among the lines I have written
before, my own darkness, brief
glimpses of light and the resting
here at last; I searched
for empathy, solidarity,
yearned for hope, could I
share with you—
but this moment needs
much less, much more
than words

so, so many miles away I sit
with you and let my heart break
open for a shaft of light
to peek through; so far from you
I hold onto hope till you
can find it for your self.

Breath/Prayer

Hold.
Gasp.
Deep.
Out.

I am not done learning from
that sharp intake of delight—
be gone, unidentifiable squeezing
constriction, taking, wasting,
suffocating the fire.

In.
Ease.
Sigh.
Flow.

Defiance

for Sam and his sister Connie

Cancer was aiming to become the greatest
recruiter for Death—attack more hearts and beaten
breasts, and all the rest: "If not I, Cancer cried,
then others will still come and do the work: Death gets
you all, though you try so hard to forget." "Oh,
really?" the humans replied. "Do you not see
that we live on inside the lives of all who do
remember, who put us back together
with the pieces of our stories? Take us,
do your worst, though we will fight to stop
you stopping lives before their time; take us,
and we will remake us ever more. For the more
you make us fear, the stronger we become;
determined to embrace the living we are given, eke it out
to one more moment, memory saved, more
ways of being grateful. We will learn
from your looming, to step out from the glooming:
be not then surprised to see us find
new ways to duck beyond your bony finger tips, however
tightly we are held within your grip; be not
amazed if we do grasp a victory each time a prize
you try to claim. So we will teach you the one
sure thing to keep us from defeat: one thing
that will resist and not be taken, though we may
fall, will each one breathe no more; one thing will live
beyond and take us with it, will carve those hollows
in Death's eyes, make lies of that inevitability
of our lives, will keep us living—and that one thing?
Is Love. Yes, Love; for Love, you see, sleeps not—not ever.
Love weathers all your cloudy rainy days, your
moonless nights; Love watches, guards and searches
for the lost among the wolves; Love connects the next,
the kin, the friend, the loved and not even you, nor
Death, can take the love that death releases from a heart
no longer beating, while other hearts beat on."

a generous turn

As I turned the corner where you were standing,
waving pamphlets at passers by, silent,
but with a loud stare, I stopped
myself from giving you the benefit of my
wisdom. I could not stop the thoughts, the
what do you hope to achieve with that waving
of pamphlets, even the giving of pamphlets
or someone's reading of your pamphlet; and
why waste your energy standing on a frozen
street corner waving pamphlets—do you realise
you are not commanded to save the world, but
to love?

Why not love?
Why do you not spend your energy
and passion building relationships with people,
rather than waving at them from street corners in assault
with accusation that we are wrong, assumption
that you are right, have one righteous, true
and holy path unto salvation?

Are you afraid? Do you fear that the God you put
your faith in might not be up to task, that
your salvation might be withdrawn when God
discovers you do not deserve it; that others might
be missing out on life in fuller richness?

As I turned the corner silent in my thinking,
God was speaking—why not love? The message
from the story told in church on Sunday
began its work on Monday as I waved away
your pamphlets and stopped resenting
your standing on the corner, to give thanks
for your presence on that corner, waving God
under the noses of pedestrians who might not

notice without such irritation that might
one day produce a pearl of wonder if one
wonders what it was that put you on
the corner of that city street one morning,
and find their way to life in fuller richness.

Two Foot London Lament

we did not like the plane trip,
the sitting, the pressure, the waiting
for touchdown on her side of the world

we did not like the hard work,
pounding gravel, grass and asphalt in search
of history and memories not your own

we did not like the air here, thick
and warm and heavy with
a summer we do not recognise

and so we bulged our skin to
stretching, we throbbed and wept,
tore ourselves to shreds—

how did you like that?

you leapt, heart, you wept, eyes,
on landing beside your sister,
distance ten months untouched

you stretched, mind, you sighed, voice,
at monuments from and for
the people important to your people

you smiled, mouth, you healed, soul,
lungs giving voice the breath
to share stories with one so well known

and so we received the balm, the careful
touch and restful moments; we took the blood
enriched; we sighed gratitude for carrying us here—

how we love all that.

on the bus: 1

matching black tops,
trousers, her nails,
specs, boots and piercings
a deeper commitment
to the theme; behind
her blue hair and tartan
scarf, his clean
business cut, their front
seat for the view, suddenly
I miss my dad, who looks
beyond my earrings and blue
feather tattoo.

A New Aunt's Gaze

I look at you
and I see your mum
who I held in my arms
as I hold you now,
three long decades ago,
only yesterday

I look at you and I see
your dad, my brother
now in the law of love
forever and always

I look at you in
flashes across my screen,
saving moments, crossing oceans
between us and we
are together again

I look at you, most
wonderful creature
I ever beheld, and whatever
felt frozen is suddenly
puddles at my boots—
look at you, miracle, gifted
reminder of all that is worth
holding on to, look
at you!

museum of art: impression

six steps down into stifling freedom from conditioned
air shared with a bus load, onto asphalt shimmering,
bodies glistening in the yellow haze.

we walk amidst all that White—stones
and crosses, House and Hill-top dome;
take in the grey and beige Smithsonians
reaching out from *that* patch of green.

I want the one at this end, in two
parts connected beneath the road, I want this home
for canvas more alive than copious flat calendar pages
gathering dust in a drawer, corners torn
from life's turning;

I want the whispered confessions of whisked
purple peaks and pink troughs flicked and brushed
with a look of having just been completed.

Let me bathe in these dappled impressions
of lilies and lakesides, bask rather in this artist's
low light than sun's bright unrelenting; let me dive
into the still silent air and solitude in the company
of tea-drinking women, parasols popping, petticoats floating
up as they sit beneath willow trees; or a family
at Christmas, champagne fizz and fireside
crackle.

                    In the garden
I write to mum, for my cup runs
over and other clichés of joy in abundance, insisting
on bubbling onto the page; a ballerina tapping en pointe
over the floorboards of my soul; a song sung deep,
deep within just loud enough to echo
in a twinkle and a smile,
and the occasional, audible, sigh.

Nanna's House

one bite
and I'm a time traveller—
1980s Adelaide—even from back
here the hint of a breeze
carries the ocean up the hill and through
the door screening flies
and streaming sunshine; my mind
walks me through front
hall (that yellow stool!), past bedroom
doors and wooden floors, green
bath, black tiles, skylight and ancient
stereo, heavy velvety curtains that cocoon
a cool retreat come midday; tennis balls
fly across another screen and I will
add another piece to the puzzle
on the dining room table, later. For now,
right here, head bowed I stand, now raise
my glance from grey-speckled lino, to rickety
flimsy painted white bench, the walls
dressed in green and blue rounded
squares, the air sings with the sugar
contained in orange-lidded Tupperware,
three white tubs of anticipation—but first,
turn, before she fades, drink
her in as she nods—just one—then too
soon tumbling back I grab a piece
of memory to keep after I've eaten
all the ginger nuts.

on being found

haikus after Luke 15

ninety-nine sheep left
stronger together: one all
alone, carried home

in darkness hidden
potential enlightenment
one shimmering coin

dying of hunger
endured unseen, nourishment:
tale of two brothers

Into One Spirit

on baptism

it runs, it frolics, it drives a path
into the earth
slowly deeper
quickening keeper of the roots
furrowed alongside
from the profligate scattering
of seeds some time ago
      it runs
a way both following
and beckoning, responding
and calling
      it runs
           alone
yours alone
and yet
      it joins
a river running far beneath all rivers
earth and ocean
      it joins
           you
to the source of all running
water makes you daughter
of the mother of us all
it runs and
         catches you up
for the ride of your life!

Joy to the whole world

may peace be with us all

Whatever your tradition,
however you are faithful,
whether in by open fire, or
out by barbeque flame,
in this season of celebration
may all that is sacred inspire
and delight you, comfort
and nurture you, challenge
and encourage you, human
beloved, living on this one
precious earth we all share.

Dream

Perchance

The Niagara whirlpool where
my stomach should be rages,
weeks before the Big Stage.

I cannot sleep.

Treetop twittering will not dim,
but spills to willfully engulf the whole,
stumped, fallen, unable to let go.

I cannot sleep.

The heavens' expanse is empty
of little diamond beams to fly
towards, reach for, soar upon—

I cannot sleep, will
not sleep, not
relinquish and submit—
but oh, how I want
to dream.

when my own voice falters

listening to the women who believe in me

you told me "you are awesome"; I will
take that hat and wear it, play
that role 'til I believe it of myself without
the costume

you told me "you are excellent at all
you do"; I will strap those laces and stride
in borrowed boots until I find
my own again

you told me "you inspire me with your
resilience"; I will wield my sword left
handed leaving cuts and bruises
free to heal

you told me "I appreciate
your vulnerability"; I will remain
on centre stage, not seeing all
those empty seats

you told me "you will be ok, you
always are"; and I believe you,
for on this you are always
right

you told me "have no fall back
plan"; and so I fall—in desperation
spread my wings and learn
to fly

For she has been a benefactor to many

A giver of gifts when joy was needed;
builder of shelter when walls fragmented;
enabler of dreams, when wings were clipped;
bestower of bounty onto stripped tables;
provider of comfort when tears surged;
filler of purses, exhausted of income;
restorer of hope in the face of despair—
she has been a benefactor to many,
one and the same Spirit in her,
in you, benefactor to me, also.

if one falls in the Forest of Dreams

would it be like a tree
falling in an unpeopled forest,
no one to bear witness but
the ground from which the roots
tear, to which the branches
smash without ceremony,
so that the tree wonders
if it really fell at all?

but the trees, the fellow trees
surely notice the air touch
roots through the broken earth,
the sun warm leaves through
gaping canopy, their branches
slapped in falling passing tumble?

Surely the trees bear witness
to the falling, the passing
life from their midst, do not
remain unchanged? Is it so?

hung out

I waited
and I waited
for the package to arrive,
but yet again it failed
in distribution, halted,
arrested I remain
                I waited
and I waited for the package
to arrive, the parcel
with the gift inside,
to grant me my reward,
a simple wish that I might
thrive
        I waited and I
waited
           day upon lengthening
day in this northern distance;
although it seemed that all
the dawning
was ceaseless dreary bleak

I waited and I waited
for a package to arrive:
it did not come,
now I am gone,
faded
with the light.

her heart's not in it

baggage unpacked from
capacity now strewn
across foreign floor

Resignation.

I do not want to be a poet any more: this food
that fills only gnaws from inside
and I am hungry all the time.

I no longer want this poet gig
in which I create a thing
of beauty that only causes
editors to gag
            and trample

on my poet words, my poet
soul in self-righteous
pitying condescension; I will
not be not good enough

any longer, no more mediocre;
obscurity
            embrace me.
The poet's life is shit and I
will have none of it,

its nothing and never and no;
I'm done with its trying to
be clever and not quite
achieving it; the judgment,

rejection, submission and self-
flagellation—
            I quit.
                I resign
the commission that was never
forthcoming anyway.

So take it back, your Divine Gift:
remove it from my DNA,

cut out the poetry, its pain
I can no longer endure.

I do not see the point of me
as poet, what is the gain
from all these words, from
speaking from the edge to a

centre deaf and dumb?
do the poems change
anything for the better?
                                    I can
not tell. I cannot tell.

I do not wish to be a poet
any more. No more. Please
take the poetry away.
Let me live another day.

average

there are no awards
for the fighters of black
dogs and demons, no extra
recognition for getting work
done before the deadline
when you've been a blip above
flatline the whole time;
and it's not much of a feather,
the crumpled stick in your
weathered cap; no one notes
your salute in the general
direction of grant-givers
blind of imagination,
when you did it anyway,
the hard way; no one sees
the darkness – for it is dark,
pet, and you belong
to the shadows, the hallows
deathly, you, always a tiny
blip on a muted screen
in an unlit room, groomed
for better, if you could get
there, weren't strapped here
between the dim hue
and the deep blue, invisible,
forgettable, but still a blip
above

taking all you've granted

sometimes I take for granted
the space and time I have for dreaming,
the means to make my way
towards those dreams, the cheer
squad's banners and buckets of gold

sometimes I take for granted
the space and time for dreams,
such luxury never dreamed of
in bunkers, tents and leaky boats
of refuge, freedom dared to come

sometimes I take for granted
walls and windows, curtains, heated
floor and safe warm bed,
fruit juice and ice cream, eggs
and potatoes and milk

sometimes I take for granted
the roof overhead, overhearing
nothing of the street-sleeping cries
for change, starvation
feeding gutters running dry of all compassion

sometimes I take for granted
telephone, computer, satellite
connection, the postcard posted
through the door, unlocking
isolation's padlock on the mind

sometimes I take for granted
connection to the world and Love,
assume you know that I am
and never showing, not performing
a response more worthy of the gift

Observing the trees: Autumn

As I note the leaves' changing colours,
I wonder—do they change colour in anticipation
of the shortening of the days, or
do the smaller hours of sunshine bring
about the fading colour, detachment
from the branch?

As I note the trees' undressing in
preparation for the lean times, I wonder—
how I might embrace the seasons of endurance
with trust and abandon, with hope
for the returning of the sun?

a prophet's homecoming

reflecting on the story from Mark 6:1–13

> withering welcome
> family ties matted, fraying
> disturbing the dust

chase the wild goose

alight
arise
soar
fly
with flight inspired
like singing choir
and life contained no more
lift the roof
on organ wings
speak
pray
praise
with tongues
alight
with Spirit blaze
trail behind a smoky
haze
these fiery days
disturbed
disturbing
comfortable no more
unsettled
ruffled
alight now, soar
arise, take flight,
each one fly,
fly high, dream wide
your uncommon gifts inspired
live life uncontained
with the goose—wild and free

I am ready

slow crack in the deep dark
unfold
      stretch
           reach
                peek
through the surface leaves
the sun pulls and pulls
long hands warm
midwifing new life
pause
      reach
           stretch
                breathe
sunlight moonlight cloudburst
small wings bear witness
the new birth
           rebirth
                bold
petals unfurl and sing!
here
    here
        here
           I am!

I am ready
        stretch
              reach
for stars sparkle from deep
within

carried: home

I walked with a dusty gold star,
one of the fallen flakes
leaving the arms of the ones
who gave them life; she showed
me the last of the brushes, singing
to the wind and the wide blue sky;
then I let her go and we each
took flight.

www.ingramcontent.com/pod-product-compliance
Lightning Source LLC
Chambersburg PA
CBHW061512040426
42450CB00008B/1582